The Tree of Life Bible Study:

Finding Healing in Jesus

Dr. Emily Hervey

Scripture quotations taken from the New American Standard Bible® (NASB), Copyright © 1960, 1962, 1963, 1968, 1971, 1972, 1973, 1975, 1977, 1995 by The Lockman Foundation. Used by permission. www.Lockman.org

All contents of THE HOLY BIBLE, NEW INTERNATIONAL VERSION®, NIV® Copyright © 1973, 1978, 1984, 2011 by Biblica, Inc.

All contents of the Common English Bible (CEB) Web Site are: Copyright 2012 by Common English Bible and/or its suppliers. All rights reserved.

Cover designed by Emily Hervey. Photos of the tree and the rings of the tree taken by Emily Hervey.

The Tree of Life Bible Study: Finding Healing in Jesus

Copyright © 2020 Emily Hervey

Worldwide Writings

ISBN-13: 978-0-9852917-6-1

Chandler, AZ

All rights reserved

Table of Contents

Introduction 3

Lesson 1: The Hidden History 7

SECTION 1: ROOTS

Lesson 2: Healthy Relational Roots 15

Lesson 3: Healing Relational Roots....................... 21

Lesson 4: Healthy Spiritual Roots 29

Lesson 5: Healing Spiritual Roots.......................... 35

Lesson 6: Healthy Emotional Roots 41

Lesson 7: Healing Emotional Roots 47

SECTION 2: HEALING

Lesson 8: Suffering—The Damaged Tree............... 55

Lesson 9: Offering Loving in Loss 63

Lesson 10: Caring for the Broken Tree 71

Lesson 11: Stopping Disease and Decay................ 79

Lesson 12: True Healing 89

Appendix A: The Immanuel Approach 97

Introduction

Purpose of the Bible Study

The *Tree of Life* Bible Study series is about discovering the fullness of LIFE: it is about thriving, not just surviving, and helping others do the same.

In this series we explore the three key components to living an abundant life:
- Connecting with the Source of Life
- Discovering your own identity, places for growth, and opportunities for healing
- Growing in relationships with others

The previous **Introduction to the Tree of Life** Bible Study (five lessons) presented the biblical significance of trees: a beautiful representation of life. Trees are used throughout Scripture in prophecies, psalms, promises, and parables. There are references to roots, branches, and fruit, as well as whole trees. We explored the references to "the Tree of Life," the presentation of the Holy Spirit as Living Water, the presentation of Jesus as the Light of the world, and an opportunity to encounter Jesus.

This study will explore the areas in our lives that are healthy and those in need of healing. Well-being is not just about what other people see on the surface in our appearance and actions. Like a tree, we have deep roots, the foundation of who we are in our relationships with others, our emotions, and our relationship with God.

We will also look at what damages a tree, causing brokenness or decay. In our own lives we face areas of grief and trauma and often need to find healing for what has happened in the past. We also learn how to help others in the storms of life.

In the first Bible Study, the Immanuel Approach was introduced. During this study, hopefully the leader or facilitator will help members experience this form of connecting with Jesus. He is the ultimate source of healing, the bringer of truth, redemption, and wholeness.

Community and Individual Time

While this Bible study can be done independently, it is ideally a combination of group discussion and personal reflection. Life and love are all about relationships. Therefore, engaging others in the learning process is key not only for the sake of learning from each other, but also creating a safe place to practice what is being discussed, allow vulnerability, mutually support one another, and offer accountability.

To facilitate these outcomes, it is optimal to create a group that stays together from beginning to end, rather than a fluid attendance of different people each lesson. If it is not feasible to go through the whole Bible study in one group, it can also be broken down by the two sections (Roots and Healing), allowing some change between them.

There is also significant value in spending individual time with God. Each lesson ends with a "Take Home" section for each individual to complete between group sessions. Setting aside personal time is not always easy; it requires effort and intentionality. Therefore, it is important to make a decision ahead of time of how to create room in your schedule and then keep each other accountable. Starting group sessions with an opportunity to share what has come out of individual application is a great way to mutually encourage one another.

Note for Group Leaders

The primary goal of this and all Bible studies is to draw closer to God, and secondary outcome is to grow in relationships with one another.

To grow in our relationship with God, it is valuable to:
- Start with prayer to focus on Jesus, give thanks for what He is doing, and invite Him to work in your hearts during that meeting.
- Depend on the guidance of the Holy Spirit, even if it means not covering all the detail of each lesson.
- End in prayer, allowing time to listen to any truth He wants each individual to take home with them and apply during the week.

To grow closer to one another:
- Allow time to get to know each other at the beginning and to share with one another each week.
- Make the Bible study a safe place to share with one another. During the first session, together agree that whatever is shared will be kept confidential.
- Strive to set an example of openness, sharing both joys and struggles.
- Each week encourage one another to identify a way to apply what was discussed, and at the beginning of the next week ask each other how it went (including the "Take Home" section). This is not a place for judgment or giving advice, but it facilitates support and accountability.

Remember that every group and every individual is unique. Some people tend to dominate discussions while others need time to process internally before speaking up. At times it can be helpful to intentionally give room for those who haven't responded to do so. Try to do this without putting pressure on the quiet members or making the talkers feel like they are not valued.

The size of the group will also influence dynamics. If it is a larger group, it might be helpful to split into smaller groups (two to four people) for sharing and prayer at the end of each week. Doing so can make sharing easier for those who are hesitant to speak to the larger group.

Lesson 1: The Hidden History

Opening Questions: When looking at a tree, what can you tell from its outward appearance? What influences its size and shape?

The Bible has many descriptions of trees either growing or being uprooted and thrown in the fire. Sometimes it is a representation of a nation, sometimes a picture of an individual.

Bible Passage: Psalm 92:12-15, NASB

> The righteous man will flourish like the palm tree,
> He will grow like a cedar in Lebanon.
> Planted in the house of the LORD,
> They will flourish in the courts of our God.
> They will still yield fruit in old age;
> They shall be full of sap and very green,
> To declare that the LORD is upright;
> He is my rock, and there is no unrighteousness in Him.

Discuss:

- What does it mean for someone to "flourish" or "grow" like a tree?

  _____
  _____
  _____
  _____

- What makes a tree healthy? How does an individual's relationship with God relate to growth?

  _____
  _____
  _____
  _____

Moses: Chosen in His Weakness

From infancy Moses was not only saved from being killed like the other Israelite infants, but was nurtured first by his own mother, then by Pharaoh's daughter. He had a connection with his own people, the Israelites, and in his early position of power he tried to stand up for them, killing an oppressive Egyptian. Yet they did not recognize or accept his leadership, and with murder on his hands he fled to Midian. There he went through a time of humbling and healing, marrying into the house of a priest, and learning the humility of tending sheep. It was after forty years of growth that he encountered God in a burning bush, and despite his fears and insecurity about his own poor speech, God called him to lead the Israelites out of Egypt.

Moses encountered harsh opposition from Pharaoh in Egypt, despite the display of God's power. After leading his people out, he constantly addressed their fears and complaints. His relationship with God was unlike the rest of the people. He encountered the glory of God to the point where his own face was too bright for the people to look at him. For forty years Moses faithfully led the Israelites in the desert, receiving the law from the Lord and putting it to practice. Yet he had his own uncertainties along the way, and because of his own failure to follow instructions, he was not allowed to enter the Promised Land.

God did not select Moses for his speech or his influence; when God called him, he looked like a simple shepherd, a runaway from Egypt without the courage to go back. Moses relied fully on God's power and guidance to overcome his fear of failure and opposition by others. He had to trust fully in the Lord to be used by Him, but when in that dependent relationship, he indeed flourished like a healthy tree. His encounters with God radically transformed him, yet there were also long seasons of gradual growth to prepare him for the role he played.

Finding Healing in Jesus

Discuss:

- How does Moses compare to Psalm 92?

  _____
  _____
  _____

- What forms of growth and healing did Moses need before becoming the leader of Israel? What about after he entered that leadership role?

  _____
  _____
  _____
  _____

Roots: The Source of Joy and Pain

This Bible study will also explore our hidden roots. This part of who we are has been with us from the beginning of our lives, shaping our perception of ourselves, God, people around us, and this world. Flourishing trees require healthy roots in quality soil. But there are often deeply rooted issues that get in the way of our relationship with God and others. We will uncover both the healthy roots that bring joy, and damaged roots in need of healing.

Moses had roots shaped by his nurturing mother, the privileges and power he experienced in the care of Pharaoh's daughter, and his relationship with others of his ethnicity, all of which influenced his compassion toward another Israelite and his aggression on an Egyptian. Some of those roots positively prepared him to lead his people, but there were other components of who he was, including his pride, that needed to be changed before he was ready for that role.

The Tree of Life

Rings: The Story of Joy and Pain

Every tree has a story hiding in the rings of the trunk, what is not visible from the outside. Each inner circle records a year of the tree's life, starting in the middle and spreading outward. In a very old tree with many rings, some are wider than others, based on the amount of growth that took place. Evidence of harsh weather, droughts, and times of flourishing all lie embedded in the tree's wood.

All that is visible to others is the outer layer of the tree, the bark, which works to protect the wood, covering wounds and defending against decay. Often, we make assumptions about others just based on the outside, without knowing their stories. We also try to protect ourselves from negative judgments by making sure we look positive on the outside.

If Moses was observed for the first time after years of leading the Israelites, no one would have guessed that he grew up in Pharaoh's house, that he had killed someone, that he spent forty years tending sheep, or even that he doubted his own ability to speak! Yet all these were significant pieces of his story.

Discuss:

- What roots and rings do you notice from in the story of Moses?

_____
_____
_____
_____

- Where have you seen transformation in your own life? What forms of maturation have come more gradually?

  _____
  _____
  _____
  _____

God knows us intimately, far deeper than what others can see on the outside. He knows our mistakes and weaknesses, our hurts and hopes, our quests and questions. And He loves us just as we are! Yet He also wants to help us grow rather than stay stagnant. Jesus invites us into intimacy with Him, promising to be with us both through times of joy and seasons of sorrow. Let us get ready to encounter His truth about who we are in our brokenness, while also discovering His restorative power.

The Tree of Life

Take Home

Read: Acts 7:20-38

Reflect:

- Think about your life story. When did you have periods of growth? When were there seasons of drought or storms?
  _____
  _____
  _____

- What specific events had a significant impact on you?
  _____
  _____
  _____

Respond:

- Draw your own rings as a timeline of your life. Include the seasons and events identified above.

The Tree of Life

For a tree to grow well, it must have deep, healthy roots. Roots begin to develop from the very beginning, even though they can't be seen by others. It is the roots that absorb the needed water and nutrients. They are especially important to keep the tree alive and standing firm in the midst of a disaster, like a storm or a drought.

Our Roots

In the same way we need to have healthy "roots" to not only survive, but to thrive. Our roots are not what people see on the outside, yet are foundational to who we are.

We have three areas of roots that are closely connected:
- **Relational roots:** From the beginning of life our relationships shape who we are!
- **Spiritual roots:** Our belief systems about who God is and how we relate to Him influences whether we live in fear or hope.
- **Emotional/psychological roots:** Our thoughts and feelings shape our words and actions, so our entire lives are influenced by the truth or lies in our minds, the wounds or wholeness in our hearts.

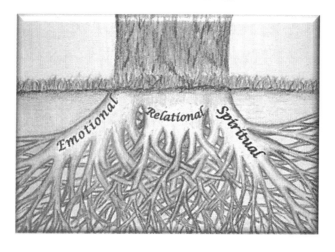

Lesson 2: Healthy Relational Roots

Opening Questions: What would happen to a tree with no roots if it were hit by a storm? What would happen to you if something horrible happened and you had no one to help you?

Bible Passage: Ephesians 3:17-18, CEB (emphasis added)

> I ask that Christ will live in your hearts through faith. As a result of having **strong roots** in love, I ask that you'll have the power to grasp love's width and length, height and depth, together with all believers.

Discuss:

- What does it mean to have strong roots in love?

  _____
  _____
  _____

- What would help us better understand, or "grasp," love?

  _____
  _____
  _____

- How does Christ's love for us relate to our love for each other?

  _____
  _____
  _____

We are made to be relational! God made us relational creatures. In the Genesis account of creation, Adam's first need (after food for survival) was a companion, for God said, "It is not good for the man to be alone" (Genesis 2:18, NASB). Humans were made in God's image, and His love for His Son and for each of us provides a template for loving relationships. Yet in our sinful human nature, selfishness obstructs pure love and patterns of broken relationships are passed from one generation to the next.

From the beginning of our lives, relationships shape our security and well-being. A baby's feeling of security in relationship with his or her mother or another caregiver directly influences how well the child's body, mind, and emotions develop.

Early family relationships also set the patterns for future relationships. Children learn from what they see around them: ways to communicate, show emotions, deal with conflict, and have overall healthy or unhealthy relationships.

Discuss:

- What do you think a healthy relationship looks like?
  _____
  _____
  _____
  _____

- Should all our relationships be the same? What might be alike or different in how we relate to others?
  _____
  _____
  _____

Jesus: The Perfect Example

Jesus spent time helping thousands of people, showing love to all. But He also had a strong support system. There was a group of men and women that followed Him closely and helped with practical needs. He chose to invest more time in 12 people, His disciples, teaching them by word and setting an example for them. Out of those 12, He had three who were closest: Peter, James, and John. They shared both what was the most amazing experience (the Transfiguration: Matthew 17:2, Mark 9:2–3, Luke 9:28–36) and the most painful ordeal (Gethsemane: Matthew 26:36-46, Mark 14:32-42).

We also need people around us who can share our joy and pain. Jesus gave us an example for supportive relationships:

1) Clear communication: From the beginning, Jesus was honest, letting His disciples know that to follow Him would mean much sacrifice. He often had to explain himself or gradually disclose more as they became better able to understand who He was, but He never deceived them.

2) Managing conflict: More than once Jesus had to deal with disputes between disciples or their disagreements with His plan. He even had to directly counter Peter's criticism (Matthew 16:22-24). But He did so openly, not with subtle sarcasm or indirect hostility, instead sharing the truth and not holding anything against them.

3) Complete acceptance: Jesus saw all the disciples' flaws and weaknesses and still loved them for who they were. He didn't wait until they had grown in maturity and knowledge, but welcomed them as they were and facilitated their learning without belittling them.

4) Vulnerability: When grieving for Lazarus, the disciples saw Him weep. When angry at the corruption in the temple, they watched Him flip tables. Jesus didn't hide His emotions or His deep thoughts; He allowed His disciples to take part, all the way to His death and resurrection.

5) Agape love: *Agape*, or unconditional love, was never something to be earned. Jesus went all the way to laying down His life for His friends, offering grace and forgiveness with no strings attached. Although we will never be able to give that same perfect love, we have an example to follow.

The Tree of Life

Discuss:

- Where did you learn how to relate to others? If you think about the people in your life who influenced you, where do you see similarities between them and your own relational patterns?

    _____
    _____
    _____

- Which healthy patterns shown by Jesus do you find come naturally to you? Which are more difficult?

    _____
    _____
    _____

We all have areas for improvement and can always look to Jesus to set an example for us to follow!

Take Home

Read: 1 Corinthians 13

Reflect:

- Review the description of love and think about the kind of love have you experienced from people around you. Write down what has given you joy.

  _____
  _____
  _____

- Consider the areas that you find difficult to live out and ask God for help.

  _____
  _____
  _____

Respond:

- How can we show agape love to others? Make a list of specific ways to show love to others this week, and each day choose one of them to do.

  _____
  _____
  _____
  _____
  _____
  _____
  _____
  _____
  _____
  _____
  _____
  _____

The Tree of Life

Lesson 3: Healing Relational Roots

Opening Questions: How would you cope if something horrible happened and you had no one to help you? Why is it important to have good relationships?

Bible Passage:

> *Ecclesiastes 4:9-12, NASB*
> Two are better than one because they have a good return for their labor. For if either of them falls, the one will lift up his companion. But woe to the one who falls when there is not another to lift him up. Furthermore, if two lie down together they keep warm, but how can one be warm alone? And if one can overpower him who is alone, two can resist him. A cord of three strands is not quickly torn apart.

Discuss:

- What might be examples of times someone falls and needs to be lifted up?

  _____
  _____
  _____

- What happens when we are alone in times of need?

  _____
  _____
  _____

- How do we create relationships where we can help each other?

  _____
  _____
  _____

It is important to have relationships where we can help one another! Yet sometimes we find it hard to let others get "too close" or we try to keep too many people close enough to feel important. It's not always easy to maintain healthy relationships, especially if we didn't learn good relationships growing up. So where do we need to be careful?

Sarai and Hagar: Seeking Worth in Fertility

Many cultures emphasize the significance of bearing children—their descendants. As Abram and Sarai grew older with no children, Sarai's feelings of shame and doubt for being barren led her to look for other options. She had a servant named Hagar, whom she trusted enough and felt close enough to that she tried to live through her to give Abram a child.

> *So Sarai said to Abram, "Now behold, the Lord has prevented me from bearing children. Please go in to my maid; perhaps I will obtain children through her" (Genesis 16:2, NASB).*

Perhaps Hagar felt used, valued only for her capacity to bear a child, and not given any choice in the matter. Regardless of the details, we know that once pregnant, she despised Sarai (vs. 4-5). Sarai felt that spite, added to her own insecurity and jealousy, and treated her harshly until Hagar fled to the desert. There, she encountered an angel, who told her to go back to Sarai. Running away from the relationship didn't resolve any issues. Tension between the descendants of Ishmael (Hagar's son) and Isaac (Sarai's son) have lasted even to the present day, played out between Muslims and Jews.

Despite her relational struggles with Hagar, Sarai and Abram (later called Sarah and Abraham) had some good aspects of communication in their relationship. Abraham listened to Sarah when she expressed her struggles with Hagar. They did not let the lack of children into their old age separate them. And finally, although she was understandably doubtful about the prophecy that she, at age 90, would bear a child, "by faith even Sarah herself received ability to conceive, even beyond the proper time of life, since she considered Him faithful who had promised" (Hebrews 11:11, NASB).

Discuss:

- How did Sarai's view of her self-worth and security influence her relationship with Hagar?

  _____
  _____
  _____
  _____
  _____

- How do you think the relationship between the two mothers influenced the relationship between their sons?

  _____
  _____
  _____
  _____

Improving Relationships

1) Setting boundaries: There are two extremes to setting boundaries. On one end, those who isolate themselves let no one near their deep thoughts and emotions. Some may be obvious "loners," while others might appear to have an abundance of friends, but never let anyone past a superficial façade. Distancing may stem from fear of abandonment if weaknesses are exposed, avoidance of pain from the potential loss of a close relationship, or guilt when feeling like a "burden" to others. For some it may just be a lack of ability to express one's heart, coming from a setting where vulnerability and revealing one's emotions were unacceptable.

On the other end of the spectrum are those who do not know how to set any boundaries. They rely on others for any sense of identity or self-worth, making them always in need of attention and affirmation. When those needs are not met or the demands are too much for the person on the other side of the relationship, the individual may push someone away or use hurtful words and actions to retaliate. Others try to earn friendships by always giving and trying to please others, never being able to say "no," and easily overloaded by requests from others. Someone who was starving for love as a child did not learn how to give and receive love in a healthy reciprocal relationship.

Although many people fall somewhere in the middle, any painful event or lack of love can influence our tendencies to either withdraw and be "safe" or to push for acceptance, even if in subtle ways. The commonality is that these approaches to relationships are based on ourselves—our needs, fears, and desires—rather than on love. For Sarah, her insecurity and lack of children made her first reach out to Hagar, then reject her out of jealousy and her desire to be loved by Abraham.

Discuss:

- Where are your boundaries? Do you allow some into your inner circle? Or do you find it difficult to let others see the "real" you? Do find security in your own identity, or do you pull everyone as close as you can and rely on them to find value?

  _____
  _____
  _____
  _____
  _____

- Is there a safe relationship where you can be vulnerable, receiving and giving both acceptance and accountability?

  _____
  _____
  _____
  _____

2) Better communication: Relationships rely on quality communication, including expression of love and management of conflict. They depend on skills of listening and observing as much as on speaking and demonstrating. People are all different, making disagreements inevitable. Without being able to understand one another and find resolutions, conflict will either be hidden where frustration festers into bitterness, or will escalate to the point of severely damaging a relationship. This is what happened with Sarah and Hagar, who originally may have had a positive enough relationship for Sarah to let her marry Abraham. But that went downhill when they both let bitterness fester, which was unfortunately never resolved.

The ability to communicate and receive love is also complicated by differences. We must be willing to go outside our comfort zones to give and receive love. This is an even steeper learning curve for those who didn't receive or witness genuine love while growing up.

Finally, mutual vulnerability is essential for communication. Sharing one's heart can easily fall outside our comfort zones, and it is even more difficult to take that step twice if it is not accepted, affirmed, and reciprocated by the other person. Without such transparency, a relationship remains relatively superficial, never reaching its maximum potential to be a place of deep love. Sarah and Abraham had plenty of faults in their marriage, but were able to communicate with each other, and together have faith in the promise of the birth of Isaac.

Discuss:
- How do you respond to conflict? Do you try to pretend there isn't a problem? Do you react strongly to frustration?

_____
_____
_____
_____

- How well do you listen to the other side of the story? Can you see things from the other person's perspective?

  _____
  _____
  _____

- When looking at your relationships with those closest to you, can you describe what makes them feel loved? Do you feel comfortable sharing each other's strengths and weaknesses?

  _____
  _____
  _____

Relational patterns are rooted in childhood, based on what we learned from our families and those around us. Sometimes we need to "unlearn" things.

Solving problems in existing relationships requires both sides to contribute! But be ready to focus on what changes **you** can make, not what the other person "should" do.

Finding Healing in Jesus

Take Home

Read: 1 John 4:7-21

Reflect:

- Look at the most important relationships in your life. When facing difficulties, do you share them with others, hide them, or depend on others to resolve them? Are there unresolved areas of hurt or conflict?

  _____
  _____
  _____

- As you think about your relationship, look at the boundaries you've set (or not set). Are there any ways those boundaries might improve?

  _____
  _____
  _____

Respond:

- Choose your top one or two relationships. Write down specific ways the relationships could improve. For each of them, think of what you could do to better understand, communicate with, and show support for that person.

  _____
  _____
  _____
  _____
  _____
  _____
  _____
  _____
  _____
  _____

The Tree of Life

Lesson 4: Healthy Spiritual Roots

Opening Questions: What do you think of when you hear someone is a "strong believer"? When might our faith be tested?

Bible Passage: Colossians 2:6-7, NASB

> Therefore as you have received Christ Jesus the Lord, so walk in Him, having been firmly rooted and now being built up in Him and established in your faith, just as you were instructed, and overflowing with gratitude.

Discuss:

- What does it look like to be firmly rooted in Christ? Built up in Him?

  _____
  _____
  _____
  _____

- How can gratitude come from our relationship with Christ? How could we express that gratitude and appreciation?

  _____
  _____
  _____
  _____

Spiritual well-being is based on our faith being firmly grounded.

Faith is relational! It comes from God's love for us and our love for God. This can create a cycle of growing deeper in our relationship with God:

This relationship is the only place to find nutrients for healthy spiritual life. Healthy spiritual roots are about being **immersed in God's love**. There we encounter His joy, peace, and hope.

Jesus repeatedly emphasizes the importance of being in His love, and the depth of that love was demonstrated by laying down His life (John 15). The result is the fruit of showing love to others, which is the essence of His calling to the disciples. That again shows the close link to the roots of relationships.

The Heroes of Faith: When Promises Don't Seem to be Fulfilled

Being rooted in Christ also gives us **hope from an eternal perspective**. Hebrews 11 describes those often known as "heroes of faith." Some saw amazing outcomes in the present (Abraham, Moses, Rahab, Gideon, etc.). They

> "...by faith conquered kingdoms, performed acts of righteousness, obtained promises, shut the mouths of lions, quenched the power of fire, escaped the edge of the sword, from weakness were made strong, became mighty in war, put foreign armies to flight" (vs. 33-34).

Yet many appeared to live in defeat:

"They were stoned, they were sawn in two, they were tempted, they were put to death with the sword; they went about in sheepskins, in goatskins, being destitute, afflicted, ill-treated" (vs. 37).

At the time, any faithful prayers for deliverance seemed to go unanswered. "All these, having gained approval through their faith, <u>did not receive what was promised</u>" (vs. 39).

Discuss:
- When hearing of "strong faith," do you associate that with seeing promises fulfilled or believing even when prayers are not being answered?

  _____
  _____
  _____

- How does this chapter compare to statements such as, "If you have enough faith, you will be healed" or "God will bless you if you have faith in Him"?

  _____
  _____
  _____

- What causes faith to grow or be strengthened?

  _____
  _____
  _____

Instead of basing our faith on immediately answered prayers and promises, we can hold on to the eternal outcome.

Think of our time on earth compared to eternity:

```
════════╫═══════════════════════════════►
   Time on earth              JOY FOR ETERNITY
```

It is only a tiny dot on an eternal timeline!

> *Life on earth is very short!*
> *What is most important is how it will precede our*
> *lives for eternity.*

Deeply rooted faith is critical in times of suffering. The love of God may not seem obvious during trials. When facing loneliness and defeat we easily question God's love and presence. In hardship, spiritual roots either give up and shrivel, or dig even deeper for God's love, becoming more firmly planted by relying on God rather than on circumstances.

Discuss:

- In the midst of difficult or painful times, do you find yourself growing closer to God or pulling away from Him?

  _____
  _____
  _____

- How might suffering look different if viewed as a place of learning dependence on God and experiencing His love?

  _____
  _____
  _____

- Can you hold on to eternal hope, even if not fulfilled in the present?

  _____
  _____
  _____

Our healthy spiritual roots are based on the loving relationship we have with God.

Finding Healing in Jesus

Take Home

Read: John 15: 1-17

Reflect:

- Look at your relationship with Jesus. On a scale of 1 to 10, how close to Him do you feel?
- Draw a representation of your relationship with Him.

- Write down anything in your own life that might make it difficult to trust Him or see His love. This might include theological questions you're struggling with, negative emotions toward Him, or simply feeling distant from Him.

  _____
  _____
  _____
  _____

- Write down any times you've witnessed or experienced His love and hope.

  _____
  _____
  _____

Respond:

- Express to God your questions, doubts, and struggles. Then specifically express appreciation for the times you have seen Him at work in your life. Spend some time seeking His Presence and listening to Him. Write down whatever comes to mind.

This process may also be done with a facilitator using the first part of the Immanuel Approached (introduced in the first Bible Study).

Lesson 5: Healing Spiritual Roots

Opening Question: What might prevent spiritual roots from being healthy or growing deeper?

Jesus told the parable of seeds falling on different soils and growing or shriveling in different places. He explained the meaning to his disciples:

Bible Passage: Matthew 13:18-23, NASB

> "Hear then the parable of the sower. When anyone hears the word of the kingdom and does not understand it, the evil one comes and snatches away what has been sown in his heart. This is the one on whom seed was sown beside the road. The one on whom seed was sown on the rocky places, this is the man who hears the word and immediately receives it with joy; yet he has no firm root in himself, but is only temporary, and when affliction or persecution arises because of the word, immediately he falls away. And the one on whom seed was sown among the thorns, this is the man who hears the word, and the worry of the world and the deceitfulness of wealth choke the word, and it becomes unfruitful.
> And the one on whom seed was sown on the good soil, this is the man who hears the word and understands it; who indeed bears fruit and brings forth, some a hundredfold, some sixty, and some thirty."

Discuss:

- What might it look like to not understand the "word of the kingdom"?

_____
_____
_____

- Think of examples of rocky places and thorns. Have you seen that in anyone's life?

_____
_____
_____

Lack of Understanding: A Distorted View of God

The original perception of God comes from what children are taught at a young age, an image presented by the culture, community, and family. It is not always accurately showing His love.

God might look wrathful, condemning and punishing sin. Children might be threatened that God would punish them for mistakes made. Fear may have been used in harshly disciplining misbehavior, sometime to an unhealthy level of threats and violence.

God might look detached when described as holy and thus separated from inferior human beings. Perhaps He did not appear to be present in times of pain, and so must not truly care.

Views of God can also be shaped by children's views of their parents or authority figures in broken families. When "father" means someone abusive, detached, or abandoning, it might be difficult to believe in a Heavenly Father who shows love and grace. The deeply ingrained views of God based on childhood wounds require identifying and confronting the source of the negative thoughts and emotions toward God.

Thorny and Rocky Soil: When Faith Is Shallow

Some hope to find immediate gratification in Jesus. They may have tried other methods of finding happiness (wealth, drugs, relationships for pleasure, etc.), but continued to feel empty. With the focus being on selfish desires, the soil cannot be tilled, preventing true life in Christ from being embraced. Superficial faith cannot withstand adversity; it is based on immediate gratification rather than eternal hope. Deeply rooted faith requires willingness to suffer for Christ's glory. That is often where true unity with Him is encountered, as the required reliance on Him leads to experiencing His grace and love.

Discuss:

- How does your culture and family present the nature of God?

    _____
    _____
    _____

- How accurate do you think your view of God is? Do feelings like guilt or self-condemnation ever make it difficult to believe in His grace and redemption?

    _____
    _____
    _____

- What first attracted you to Jesus? Is it the same reason you follow Him now?

    _____
    _____
    _____

Saul: The Transformation of Spiritual Roots

There was once a man named Saul, who had deep, but unhealthy spiritual roots. To him, God was detached, accessible only through good deeds, not based on a personal relationship. His faith was shallow, but he enjoyed showing off how "religious" he was. He earned respect in his community for his apparent zeal for God, but his faith was not being tested; instead it gave immediate gratification. When he encountered Jesus directly, he learned the truth about His love.

The Tree of Life

After his dramatic conversion, his relationship with Jesus became the center of his life and ministry. When times of trouble came, Paul (as he was known among Gentiles) showed a healthy faith. While his relationship with Christ started in a complete shift in perspective, he spent the rest of his life growing in faith and love for Christ. As Paul grew closer to Jesus, he learned to depend more fully on His strength and guidance. When he preached, it was the Holy Spirit speaking through him. When he wrote letters to the churches, the words were divinely inspired and were constantly pointing believers back to Jesus. When he faced persecution, only his connection with Jesus was enough to help him rejoice in the midst of suffering. Paul set an example of trusting God for His work in him and through him.

Discuss:

- What can we learn from Paul's transformation?
  _____
  _____
  _____

- How did his image of God change? What about his relationship with Jesus?
  _____
  _____
  _____

- How were his relational and spiritual roots connected?
  _____
  _____
  _____

God is the Gardener

God was the one who transformed Paul. Jesus said, *"I am the true vine, and my Father is the gardener. He cuts off every branch in me that bears no fruit, while every branch that does bear fruit He prunes so that it will be even more fruitful"* (John 15:1-2, NIV). The tree doesn't decide which parts need pruning or watering. Likewise, we must follow God's lead: He is the source of living water and light of truth, and He knows everything about us. God is *always* better than we are at bringing healing, peace, and joy!

The Tree of Life

Take Home

Read: Romans 8:1-17

Reflect:

- How easy is it for you to depend fully on God and His transformation?
  _____
  _____
  _____

- Are there any areas where you like to feel in control?
  _____
  _____
  _____

- Are there any areas where you are worried about your own possible failure?
  _____
  _____
  _____

Respond:

- Spend some time asking God to help you release each of those areas identified into His hands.

This process may also be done with a facilitator using the Immanuel Approached (introduced in the first Bible Study).

Finding Healing in Jesus

Lesson 6: Healthy Emotional Roots

Opening Question: What makes us able to withstand stress and trauma?

As children, we develop our ways to deal with challenges and pain, begin discovering our identity and purpose in life, and learn to process thoughts and emotions, both positive and negative ones. We are shaped largely by our interactions at home and in the community.

Bible Passage: Hebrews 12:14-15, NASB

> Pursue peace with all men, and the sanctification without which no one will see the Lord. See to it that no one comes short of the grace of God; that no <u>root of bitterness</u> springing up causes trouble, and by it many be defiled.

Discuss:

- Where does a root of bitterness come from?

- How can grace impact us?

- What might be the effects of growing up surrounded by grace and peace? How does that compare to growing up without learning how to find healing and forgiveness?

Joseph: Resilience from the Roots

Although he had problems with his brothers, Joseph was loved by his father, who listened to him and showed care by giving him a colorful coat. Receiving visions and later interpreting the visions of others suggested he had a good relationship with God. From when he was a young man, he faced extreme suffering: his brothers almost killed him, he was sold into slavery, and he spent years in prison for a wrong he did not commit. Yet, he handled each situation trusting God. At each point in Egypt his godliness led to good relationships, earning him favor, and eventually, through his interpretation of dreams and wise leadership, he ruled all of Egypt! (See Genesis 37, 39-45.)

Discuss:

- What do you think your reactions (feelings, words, and actions) would have been if you had Joseph's experience of rejection—to the point of almost being killed—by people close to you?

  _____
  _____
  _____

- How do you think Joseph managed being sold into slavery, facing false accusations, and spending years wondering if he would ever get out of prison?

  _____
  _____
  _____
  _____

- What do you do to cope in times that look bleak?

  _____
  _____
  _____
  _____

Joseph showed strong emotional roots:
- ➢ **Secure identity formation:** Joseph was able to accept himself, both in strengths and weaknesses. He held on to the promise of being loved by God and his own father, even when sitting in prison. When things went well, he gave God the credit. He was secure enough to face challenges and accept responsibility at all levels in Egypt.
- ➢ **Resilience:** Joseph was able to recover and grow at each stage of adversity. He not only handled the stress and distress well, but they became opportunities to rise and become more powerful in a godly way.
- ➢ **Ability to differentiate between truth and distortions**: Joseph didn't let the words and actions of his brothers make him feel like an unwanted failure. He recognized the pain caused by his brothers, but was able to forgive them.
- ➢ **Finding hope in the love of God:** He trusted God's promises in dreams, even though they were not fulfilled for decades. He recognized God's sovereignty in both times of joy and sorrow.
- ➢ **Discovering one's purpose in serving God:** Joseph's brothers were afraid of what he might do to them in punishment, but he reframed it, telling them, "[Y]ou meant evil against me, but God meant it for good in order to bring about this present result, to preserve many people alive" (Genesis 50:20, NASB).

Our ability to handle life's struggles is closely related to how we view ourselves, whether believing we are valuable regardless of our strengths or weaknesses, or being uncertain of our own worth apart from accomplishments. Without being secure in our identity, having skills in processing (not avoiding) our emotions, and learning to grow from mistakes made, we may find it hard to deal with adversity. **Resilience**, or being able to recover and grow from difficult experiences, is related to all areas of roots. When healthy, roots can help the tree withstand tough storms.

Discuss:

- How did having strong emotional roots shape Joseph's reaction to the adversity faced?

- How might it have been different if he did not find hope in God?

- What are examples of resilience in your own life or in the lives of other people you know?

Take Home

Read: Genesis 46:3-15

Reflect:

Think about the following questions:

- How do you view yourself? Positively? Critically? Looking for areas for growth?

  _____
  _____
  _____

- Is your view consistent or dependent on recent successes/failures?

  _____
  _____
  _____

- Think of past challenges. Did you feel supported by others and free to express emotions? Were you able to grieve and find healing? Did you see any growth or learning come from it?

  _____
  _____
  _____
  _____

- What brings you hope? Do you feel you have a purpose in life?

  _____
  _____
  _____
  _____

The Tree of Life

Respond:

- Draw a representation of yourself, including where you find your identity, your strengths and weaknesses, and what has shaped you to be who you are today.

Lesson 7: Healing Emotional Roots

Opening Question: How do you think your self-esteem, your perception of your own worth, as an adult was influenced by your experiences growing up?

Young children take everything said by authority figures as truth, including negative and false messages about who they are. The results are long-lasting.

Bible Passage: Proverbs 11:29-31, NASB

> He who troubles his own house will inherit wind,
> And the foolish will be servant to the wisehearted.
> The fruit of the righteous is a tree of life,
> And he who is wise wins souls.
> If the righteous will be rewarded in the earth,
> How much more the wicked and the sinner!

Discuss:

- How might someone "trouble his own house" in the emotional and spiritual areas of life?

- What are the results of abuse in the home?

- How can parents be righteous in a way that brings life to their families?

Understanding Unhealthy Emotional Roots

We all develop how we view ourselves from the messages we hear when growing up, whether loving or unloving. When feeling unloved, rejected, blamed, or inferior, children adopt the messages received about never being "good enough" or being unworthy of attention. These beliefs are deeply rooted and distorted views that shape our interpretation of all that happens in life and relationships. Small mistakes trigger the thought that "I can never do things right." An inconsiderate word from a friend is interpreted as "Nobody likes me."

Negative beliefs come with an overall feeling of shame, because we live in a sinful world. The distorted view of a person's identity creates patterns of mistrust, dependence on those around them, alienation from the world, or seeking to be the center of attention, trying to convince themselves and others that they are superior. These beliefs can also contribute to struggles like depression or anxiety. Not everyone has extreme feelings of abandonment, shame, or pessimism. But many of us react to negative statements more strongly than positive ones. We may want to please others, or perhaps feel the need to prove our own worth through success.

Discuss:

- Where do you find self-worth?

  _____
  _____
  _____

- When you make a mistake or something bad happens, what kind of thoughts go through your head about yourself or the situation?

  _____
  _____
  _____

- If they are negative, do you see them as broad conclusions (e.g. "I always make mistakes" or "I'm a failure") or based on fact (e.g. "I could've made a better decision, but I have also done some things well")?

  _____
  _____
  _____

- How do you respond (emotionally, cognitively, and verbally) to negative thoughts?

  _____
  _____
  _____

Jacob: From "Second Best" to the Father of the Nation

In biblical times, the firstborn son was always treated as the best, the one worthy of greater blessings and a larger inheritance. Jacob and Esau were twins, but because Esau came out first, he was considered the firstborn. Isaac loved Esau, the outdoorsman, more than Jacob, the quieter son (Genesis 25:28). Jacob likely felt put down, but found alternative ways to gain the upper hand: he bargained for the birthright when Esau was hungry for his soup (Gen. 25:31). He deceived his father to get a greater blessing (Genesis 27). Ultimately, he ran away, afraid of being killed by his brother for stealing those blessings. It took years of time apart before being able to overcome his fear of his brother, and even during that time he used deception to protect himself from his father-in-law.

When it was time to be reunited with Esau, Jacob sent many gifts ahead, hoping to get on his good side. Before facing his brother directly, he prayed, "Please rescue me from the hand of my brother Esau, for I am afraid of him; otherwise, he may come and attack me, the mothers, and their children" (Genesis 32:11). That night he wrestled with the Angel of the Lord, fighting for blessings just as he had been doing all his life, and unwilling to give up all night. This time he didn't win in the physical sense; God brought him to a place of weakness, limping with a dislocated hip. But he finally discovered God's sovereignty and blessing. "For I have seen God face to face," he said, "and I have been delivered" (vs. 30). He was renamed Israel, "because you have struggled with God and with men and have prevailed" (vs. 28).

Discuss:

- Put yourself in Jacob's shoes. How would it feel to know your father loved your brother (or sister) more than you?
  _____
  _____
  _____

- What did Jacob do to protect himself when afraid?
  _____
  _____
  _____

- How do you think the pain in Jacob's early relationships influenced his actions and emotions?
  _____
  _____
  _____

- Have you even had times when you "wrestled" with questions about God?
  _____
  _____
  _____

Our roots can be influenced by difficult experiences during childhood, when we didn't have the ability to deal directly with emotions. Like Jacob, we might try to run away from our hurt.

A fearful experience without a way to process it can precede long-term anxiety or later surfacing of bad memories. It is like a deep wound that festers until it is cleaned out, which is also a painful process. The healing process might be both in the restoring damaged relationships, and in encountering God.

The Tree of Life

Take Home

Read: Genesis 32

Reflect:

- Think about past difficult past experiences, particularly from childhood. Were there any times that you didn't feel you had closure or healing?

  _____
  _____
  _____

- Thinks of the three areas of roots: Relational, Spiritual, and Emotional. Draw or write ways those difficult experiences might have influenced each set of roots.

Respond:

- Spend some time asking God to help you release each of those experiences into His hands. It may not all happen immediately, as we often need help in the healing process, but opening your heart to let God step in is an important first step.

This process may also be done with a facilitator using the Immanuel Approached (introduced in the first Bible Study).

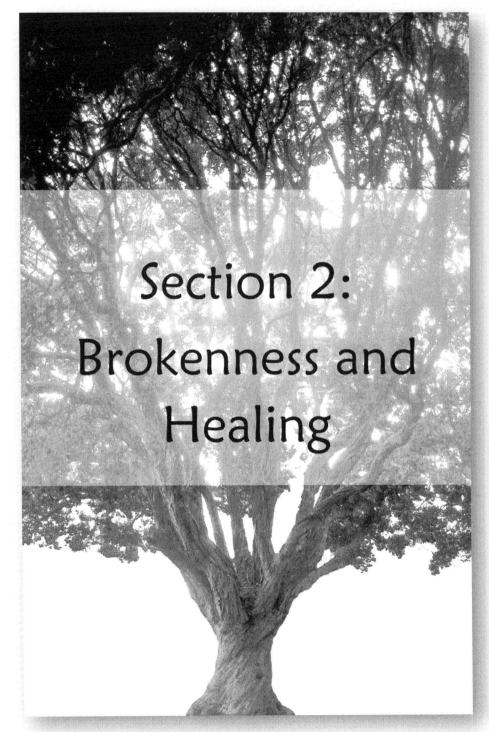

The Tree of Life

Lesson 8: Suffering—The Damaged Tree

Opening Question: Many of us have asked, "If God is loving, why it there so much suffering?" How do you respond to that?

This question is one many people have wrestled with, especially when dealing with their own struggles or those in the lives of those close to them. Job dealt with the same questions when facing multiple forms of loss and trauma. He cried out:

Bible Passage: Job 10:1-18, NASB

> "I loathe my own life;
> I will give full vent to my complaint;
> I will speak in the bitterness of my soul.
> "I will say to God, 'Do not condemn me;
> Let me know why You contend with me.
> 'Is it right for You indeed to oppress,
> To reject the labor of Your hands,
> And to look favorably on the schemes of the wicked?
> 'Have You eyes of flesh?
> Or do You see as a man sees?
> 'Are Your days as the days of a mortal,
> Or Your years as man's years,
> That You should seek for my guilt
> And search after my sin?
> 'According to Your knowledge I am indeed not guilty,
> Yet there is no deliverance from Your hand.
> 'Your hands fashioned and made me altogether,
> And would You destroy me?
> 'Remember now, that You have made me as clay;
> And would You turn me into dust again?
> 'Did You not pour me out like milk and curdle me like cheese;

Clothe me with skin and flesh,
And knit me together with bones and sinews?
'You have granted me life and lovingkindness;
And Your care has preserved my spirit.
'Yet these things You have concealed in Your heart;
I know that this is within You:
'If I sin, then You would take note of me,
And would not acquit me of my guilt.
'If I am wicked, woe to me!
And if I am righteous, I dare not lift up my head.
I am sated with disgrace and conscious of my misery.
'Should my head be lifted up, You would hunt me like a lion;
And again You would show Your power against me.
'You renew Your witnesses against me
And increase Your anger toward me;
Hardship after hardship is with me.
'Why then have You brought me out of the womb?
Would that I had died and no eye had seen me!'"

Discuss:

- What questions and complaints do you see in this passage? What emotions are expressed?

_____
_____
_____
_____

- Have you ever had similar questions? In what circumstances?

_____
_____
_____
_____

- How would you respond to Job's words?
_____
_____
_____

Job: When Life Couldn't Get Worse

Job was very well off and known to be a righteous man. There was no reason for him to be punished. When Satan challenged God that Job would only follow Him when life was easy, God knew that he would hold fast to his faith, even during the tough times. So, God allowed Job to experience suffering, so much so that he lost nearly everything: his possessions, his children, and his own health.

Job had every reason to question God, to be anguished, to be confused, and to be angry. In fact, he expressed all of those emotions, even cursing the day he was born! In the midst of his physical, emotional, and spiritual struggles, he questioned God as seen in the passage above. Yet, he did not denounce his faith in God, saying:

> "As for me, I know that my Redeemer lives,
> And at least He will take His stand on the earth"
> (Job 19:25, NASB).

At the same time, Job's friends were trying to give reason for what had happened, placing most of the blame on Job—which was neither comforting nor accurate. After allowing Job to struggle with these questions, God stepped in, reminding Job of how His power and actions were beyond what humans could see or grasp. Job was humbled, realizing he couldn't understand all God did, and repented. God restored Job with many blessings, but Job would never forget all the pain he had experienced, his encounter with God in the midst of it, and what he learned because of it. The brokenness left a memory that would never be erased, but it led to growth rather than bitterness.

The Tree of Life

Discuss:

- How do you think Job's suffering influenced his relationship with God? With his family? With his friends?
  _____
  _____
  _____

- What might he have learned about himself that he wasn't aware of previously?
  _____
  _____
  _____

- How might the outcome have been different if he had rejected God instead of bringing his struggles directly to Him?
  _____
  _____
  _____

Broken Branches

The wood from trees tells stories of grief and pain. Whenever a

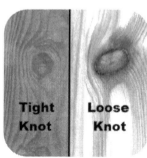
Tight Knot   Loose Knot

tree has a piece broken off, it leaves a damaged area that turns into a knot. Many times, the stubs are integrated into the living wood as the tree grows outward; these are called tight knots. In contrast, "loose knots" form around injured or dead branches, leaving decayed material or a hole inside, eventually enveloped by the wood, but still decaying.

Just as wood carries the history of times when pieces were broken off, our memories record the difficult experiences we all have had. How well we process them can lead to healing and learning or to damage.

Tight knots are integrated into the tree as living wood. These could be seen as challenging events, mistakes, or disappointments that were well-processed at the time, becoming an opportunity for learning and growth. Perhaps a child's desire was unfulfilled, but rather than causing bitterness, it became the basis for finding a creative alternative. Or maybe there was an early conflict painful at the time but resolved in a healthy way, which become a good template for dealing with future disagreements. The event might even have been more drastic. A house burned down, but the support from the family and community was more evident than ever before, and there developed a new perspective on the insignificance of material possessions. The memory of the pain faced did not disappear, but was processed in a healthy way.

In loose knots, the decay is still occurring. These knots can be symbolic of traumatic events or unresolved grief, experiences that had a lasting negative impact. Thinking back to the event is still uncomfortable, triggering negative emotions or even physical reactions. The memories and emotions may have been contained by coping mechanisms, which allowed the individual to keep functioning, but were not resolved.

Discuss:

- Do you think Job's experiences turned into tight knots or loose knots? What might have been the long-term effects?

- What are of examples of loose and tight "knots" you've seen in your life or the lives of others?

When we are in times of brokenness it is normal and healthy to experience and express our emotions. Sometimes, like Job, we can never understand all that happened (especially on a spiritual level), but can still grow from it. If we don't address the pain, fear, loss, and anger we can slip into bitterness, depression, and often unhealthy ways of coping.

Take Home

Read: Job 42

Reflect:

- Have you seen tight knots—events difficult at the time but finding healthy closure—that influenced you in a positive way?

- When looking at events that were not resolved, how did you avoid or cope with the memory? What outcomes do you see?

Respond:

- If you see those "loose knots" still in your life, think about what steps you might be willing to take to address them, and share it with someone close to you. Ask God to bring healing to those memories.

This process may also be done with a facilitator using the Immanuel Approach (introduced in the first Bible Study).

The Tree of Life

Lesson 9: Offering Loving in Loss

Opening Questions: When seeing someone else struggling with loss or trauma, how do you respond to that person? What emotional reactions do you see in yourself?

People often feel uncomfortable around someone who is clearly hurting. We often try to explain what happened, or "comfort" the person with encouraging words. Sometimes we just avoid uncomfortable conversations. We read about Job in the last lesson. He had four friends who came and were supportive for the first four days. Then they began to try to explain what had happened. It only made it harder!

Bible Passage: Job 16:2-5, NASB

> [Job said to his friends] "I have heard many such things. Sorry comforters are you all. Is there no limit to windy words? Or what plagues you that you answer? I too could speak like you, if I were in your place. I could compose words against you and shake my head at you. I could strengthen you with my mouth and the solace of my lips could lessen your pain."

Discuss:

- What are negative and positive ways people have reached out to you when you were struggling?

_____
_____
_____
_____
_____

- What are ways someone might "compose words against you"?
  _____
  _____
  _____

- Why do you think it is so easy to be judgmental, blaming the one who is suffering?
  _____
  _____
  _____

- How could words be strengthening?
  _____
  _____
  _____

We live in a broken world and everyone, at some time or another, experiences loss. There is a very real need for a chance to grieve these losses, and there is no single "right way" to do that. Often cultural expectations can affect how free traumatized individuals feel to express or process the emotions, thoughts, and beliefs that come with trauma, which can help or hurt the healing process. Grieving is a helpful way to heal from pain, and can take a long time. But if there is no place provided for grieving, the buried hurt can have a long-lasting negative impact. Often when we try to be comforting to those who are hurting, we say words that are unhelpful.

Here are some examples of words **not** to say to a grieving person:

- I know how you feel
- It was probably for the best
- He is better off now
- It was her time to go
- At least he went quickly

- You should work towards getting over this
- You are strong enough to deal with this
- You should be glad he passed quickly
- That which doesn't kill us makes us stronger
- You'll feel better soon
- It's good that you are alive
- It's good that no one else died
- It could be worse, you still have a brother/sister/mother
- Everything happens for the best according to God's plan
- We are not given more than we can bear
- *(To a child)* You are the man/woman of the house now

Most of us likely would say some of these things to be comforting, but "convincing" someone that things will get better does not help; it is trying to communicate with the mind, not the heart. What a grieving person usually needs most is someone to share the pain in his or her heart.

Jesus Wept

Jesus was close friends with three siblings: Mary, Martha, and Lazarus. When Lazarus got very sick, Mary and Martha sent a message to Jesus, asking Him to come to Bethany, hoping He would heal Lazarus (John 11). But Jesus waited, and by the time He arrived, Lazarus had already been dead for four days. Already other people were there trying to console them (vs. 19), but when they found out He was coming, Martha and then Mary each went to Him, weeping; "Lord, if you had been here, my brother would not have died." He already knew, and told Martha, that He would resurrect Lazarus, but first He shared in their sorrow.

> When Jesus therefore saw her weeping, and the Jews who came with her also weeping, He was deeply moved in spirit and was troubled, and said, "Where have you laid him?" They said to Him, "Lord, come and see." Jesus wept. So the Jews were saying, "See how much He loved him!" (John 11:33-36, NASB)

Jesus knew Lazarus would soon be raised from the dead, a display of His own power. He even told Martha that Lazarus would rise again when she asked for a miracle. Yet Jesus also showed His love by joining the sisters in their grief and weeping with them instead of telling them not to cry. He showed His own humanity, displayed the significance of close relationships, and set an example for us to follow.

Discuss:

- How do you think Mary and Martha felt when Jesus wept with them?

  _____
  _____
  _____

- How did Jesus' display of emotion change the significance of Lazarus' resurrection from the dead?

  _____
  _____
  _____

- What does this show us about the appropriate way to reach out to those who are grieving?

  _____
  _____
  _____
  _____
  _____
  _____

Every person is different in how they respond to loss and the needs they might have, so there isn't one "correct" way to help someone who is grieving. However, there are some ways to show love that can be very helpful.

Ways to show love to a grieving or traumatized person[1]:

- Acknowledge the situation.
  - Example: "I heard that your_____ died." Using a clear word like "died" shows that you are more open to talk about how the person really feels.
- Express your concern. *"I'm sorry to hear that this happened to you."*
- Be genuine in your communication and don't hide your feelings. *"I'm not sure what to say, but I want you to know I care."*
- Provide practical support. *"I'm going to the market. What can I bring you from there?"*
  - Often it is best to act on needs without waiting for the person to ask you; this reduces feelings of guilt or feeling like a burden.
- Ask how she or he feels.
  - The emotions of grief can change rapidly, so don't assume you know how the bereaved person feels on any given day.
- Accept and acknowledge all feelings, even if they seem irrational. *"It's normal to have all these feelings." "It's okay to cry or feel angry."*
- Be willing to sit in silence.
  - What is comforting is your presence, including at times when he or she doesn't feel like talking.
- Let the bereaved or traumatized person describe what happened multiple times.
  - Telling the story is a way of processing what occurred. Creating a safe place to tell the story helps the healing process.
- Offer comfort and reassurance without minimizing the loss.
  - If you have a similar loss, you may share some of your experience, but remember that everyone has unique feelings. Instead of "I know how your feel," a sentence like, "I know this can feel very painful" shows that you can relate.

The Tree of Life

Discuss:

- Which of the statements NOT to say have you heard or said? How does the list of ways to show love compare with your cultural traditions?

  _____
  _____
  _____

- Considering the differences between individuals, what might be ways to identify how to best to support someone in grief?

  _____
  _____
  _____

What is most important in helping the hurting is simply being present and listening. Times of loss are often lonely, so letting someone know that they are not alone is very valuable. Comfort means sharing pain, not erasing it.

Take Home

Read: 2 Corinthians 1:2-7

Reflect:

Read the list of ways to support someone who is grieving.

- Have you ever tried any of these or seen them put to practice? Which would be easy and which might be more uncomfortable?

    _____
    _____
    _____

- Think of difficult times you have faced in the past. What was most comforting to you?

    _____
    _____
    _____

Respond:

- If you know someone dealing with a loss, spend some time praying for them, then consider a good way to show love to them and take action.

The Tree of Life

Lesson 10: Caring for the Broken Tree

Opening Questions: What do you see people do in a crisis situation? How do responses to danger differ from one person to the next?

The prophets often had very tough jobs, telling the painful truth and predicting the disastrous results of ongoing sin. When listeners didn't take it well, the prophets received the brunt of their anger. Jeremiah was no exception, and in the midst of harsh treatment, he cried out to God.

Bible Passage: Lamentations 3:46-59, NASB

> All our enemies have opened their mouths against us.
> Panic and pitfall have befallen us,
> Devastation and destruction;
> My eyes run down with streams of water
> Because of the destruction of the daughter of my people.
> My eyes pour down unceasingly,
> Without stopping,
> Until the LORD looks down and sees from heaven.
> My eyes bring pain to my soul
> Because of all the daughters of my city.
> My enemies without cause
> Hunted me down like a bird;
> They have silenced me in the pit
> And have placed a stone on me.
> Waters flowed over my head;
> I said, "I am cut off!"
> I called on Your name, O LORD,
> Out of the lowest pit.
> You have heard my voice,
> "Do not hide Your ear from my prayer for relief,
> From my cry for help."

You drew near when I called on You;
You said, "Do not fear!"
O Lord, You have pleaded my soul's cause;
You have redeemed my life.
O LORD, You have seen my oppression;
Judge my case.

Discuss:

- What emotions do you notice being expressed? How would you describe Jeremiah's relationship with God?

　_____
　_____
　_____
　_____

- Jeremiah was distressed over both the destruction of others ("the daughter of my people") and his own fear. How are we affected by both what we witness (including in the media) and experience ourselves?

　_____
　_____
　_____

When a tree is hit hard by a storm, an earthquake, or even someone intending to harm it, significant pieces can be broken off, leaving it damaged and exposed. In the same way, when we encounter a frightening and painful event, there can be immediate and longer-term results.

The term "trauma" is defined as witnessing an actual occurrence or threat of death, serious injury, or sexual violence. Sometimes it is experienced directly, but it can also occur when witnessing it happen to someone else, hearing about it happening to a close family member or friend, or being exposed to frequent description of details (such as those helping traumatized individuals and hearing many stories).[2] Early reactions to trauma include:

Domain	Negative Responses
Cognitive	Confusion, disorientation, worry, intrusive thoughts and images, self-blame
Emotional	Shock, sorrow, grief, sadness, fear, anger, numbness, irritability, guilt, and shame
Social	Extreme withdrawal, interpersonal conflict
Physiological	Fatigue, headache, muscle tension, stomachache, increased heart rate, exaggerated startle response, difficulties sleeping
Domain	Positive Responses
Cognitive	Determination and resolve, sharper perceptions, courage, optimism, faith
Emotional	Feeling involved, challenged, mobilized
Social	Social connectedness, altruistic helping behaviors
Physiological	Alertness, readiness to respond, increasing energy

Tamar: Abuse within the Family (2 Samuel 13:1-20)

Tamar, one of King David's daughters, had a half-brother named Amnon. He lusted after her, and deceived both her and their father, David, to get her into his house, where he tried to convince her to have sex. She refused, trying to protect her virginity. "However, he would not listen to her; since he was stronger than she, he violated her and lay with her" (2 Samuel 13:14). Amnon then hated her and kicked her out of the house, where she publicly showed her loss, putting ashes on her head, tearing the clothing that symbolized virginity, and crying out loud. Her brother Absalom meant well when trying to protect her by asking her to keep it quiet, and to "not take this matter to heart" (vs. 20), even though he himself hated Ammon for violating Tamar. But keeping it silent didn't help her; she was described as "desolate." In his own anger, Absalom took revenge by killing Amnon, which brought no healing, leading to his own fleeing and more rifts in the family. Tamar went through a major trauma, but no one knew how to help her or deal with their own bitterness.

Discuss:

- What reactions do you notice in Tamar?
  _____
  _____
  _____

- What might Absalom or other family members have done to help Tamar?
  _____
  _____
  _____

Some people are able to recover quickly, especially if they have strong relational, emotional, and spiritual roots: good relationships with supportive people, healthy ways to experience and process emotions, and the ability to turn to God for help, even though questions and doubts are present. Here are some good and bad ways for someone who has experienced trauma to respond:

WHAT HELPS[3]
- Talking to another person for support or spending time with others
- Focusing on something practical that you can do right now to manage the situation better

- Engaging in positive distracting activities (sports, hobbies, reading)
- Using relaxation methods (breathing exercises, meditation, calming self-talk, soothing music)
- Getting adequate rest and eating healthy meals
- Participating in a support group
- Trying to maintain a normal schedule
- Exercising in moderation
- Scheduling pleasant activities
- Keeping a journal
- Taking breaks
- Seeking counseling
- Reminiscing about a loved one who has died

WHAT DOESN'T HELP

- Using alcohol or drugs to cope
- Working too much
- Extreme avoidance of thinking or talking about the event or a death of a loved one
- Extreme withdrawal from family or friends
- Violence or conflict
- Not taking care of yourself

Some people are unable to process their negative memories or respond in a healthy way, and the negative symptoms persist. Sometimes individuals can suppress their feelings and avoid thinking about the trauma for years, but eventually it can't be buried any longer. If it has been more than a month since the trauma and an individual is still dealing with memories, flashbacks, or nightmares and having difficulty coping, he or she may be struggling with Post Traumatic Stress Disorder (PTSD). It is **not** our job to "diagnose" it, but understanding this reaction can be helpful.

The symptoms include:[4]
- **Re-experiencing the trauma** (at least one way):
    - Intrusive thoughts
    - Nightmares
    - Flashbacks (feeling like it is happening all over again)
    - Emotional or physical distress after being exposed to something related to memory of the trauma
- **Avoiding trauma-related stimuli** (at least one way):
    - Thoughts or feelings related to trauma
    - Physical reminders of trauma
- **Worsened negative thoughts or feelings** (at least two):
    - Inability to recall key features of the trauma
    - Overly negative thoughts and assumptions about oneself or the world
    - Exaggerated blame of self or others for causing the trauma
    - Negative mood/feelings
    - Decreased interest in activities
    - Feeling isolated
    - Difficulty experiencing positive mood/feelings
- **Worsened arousal and reactivity** (at least two ways):
    - Irritability or aggression
    - Risky or destructive behavior
    - Hypervigilance
    - Heightened startle reaction
    - Difficulty concentrating
    - Difficulty sleeping

Children can also develop PTSD, although symptoms might look different, including acting like a younger child (including loss of control in areas like bed wetting), playing out violence with toys, nightmares, and physical complaints. When trauma is the cause of poor behavior, it is important that the child feels safe and loved, not condemned or punished.

It is important to first help a person with PTSD understand that they are not alone—many other people have experienced these reactions to trauma. Our bodies have a natural, God-given tendency to protect ourselves from danger. As long as the brain has not found closure to the traumatic incident, it believes danger is still imminent and remains in the defensive mode. Inviting Jesus into the memory of that event changes how the brain perceives the memory, and replaces fear with peace. The memory should not be erased, but instead is transformed into a memory of encountering Jesus. This is part of the Immanuel Approach, (see the "Introduction to the Tree of Life" Bible Study).

A simple form of the Immanuel Intervention can be used working with children: they can be very good at connecting with Jesus! If there is no improvement, finding professional help may be the best option to determine the cause of the problems.

Discuss:

- When have you noticed any of these symptoms in reaction to trauma (even if not to the point of developing PTSD)? These may be in your own lives or the lives of others.

  _____
  _____
  _____

- What are ways to show support to someone who has recently experienced trauma?

  _____
  _____
  _____

- How can we encourage the helpful ways of responding to trauma?

  _____
  _____
  _____

Take Home

Read: Lamentations 3:1-25

Reflect:

- Consider how desolate and desperate Jeremiah was when witnessing destruction.

- Have there been times when you felt upset toward God like Jeremiah did? How might you react when others who are struggling also express anger toward God and others?

_____
_____
_____

- How do you think he reached the point of finding hope? What does it look like to wait on the Lord and seek Him?

_____
_____
_____

Respond:

- If you are experiencing the symptoms of PTSD, consider having an Immanuel Approach session with a facilitator.
- If you know someone else who has been through trauma, this might be an opportunity to practice facilitating a session, if the individual is open to it. Make sure to have someone with you who has had some training.

Lesson 11: Stopping Disease and Decay

Opening Question: How do you react when hearing a story of abuse or persecution?

Hurt is most powerful when caused by someone significant in our lives. David had numerous enemies, but multiple times he fled from his own father-in-law. In many psalms he cried out to God.

Bible Passage: Psalm 143:1-6, NASB

> Hear my prayer, O LORD,
> Give ear to my supplications!
> Answer me in Your faithfulness, in Your righteousness!
> And do not enter into judgment with Your servant,
> For in Your sight no man living is righteous.
> For the enemy has persecuted my soul;
> He has crushed my life to the ground;
> He has made me dwell in dark places, like those who have long been dead.
> Therefore my spirit is overwhelmed within me;
> My heart is appalled within me.
> I remember the days of old;
> I meditate on all Your doings;
> I muse on the work of Your hands.
> I stretch out my hands to You;
> My soul longs for You, as a parched land.   Selah.

Discuss:

- Although David often feared for his physical safety, he also had internal struggles. What do you think he meant when describing his soul, spirit, and heart?

_____
_____
_____

- How did being made to "dwell in dark places" compare to being dead? Consider physical, emotional, cognitive, and spiritual factors.

    _____
    _____
    _____
    _____

- What do you notice about David's plea to God?

    _____
    _____
    _____

David: Issues with the In-Laws

David's first encounter with King Saul was one of servant to ruler, as young David volunteered to fight Goliath (1 Samuel 17). As David grew in popularity for his military victories, Saul began to feel threatened. The relationship became complex as David became close friends with Saul's son, Jonathan, and even spent time playing the harp for Saul. The violence began when Saul threw a spear at him in his own home (1 Samuel 18:1-15). David escaped, but came back, whether by choice or demand, and it happened again. Saul tried to manipulate David into dangerous situations, even through giving his daughter to David as a wife, on the condition that he first kill 200 Philistines. The plot failed when David succeeded against the odds (1 Samuel 18:17-30).

From then on there were multiple occasions when Saul tried to kill David, instilling fear and causing him to run away. Yet in David's position as a subject and son-in-law, he chose not to reciprocate when given the opportunity (1 Samuel 24, 26). He cared about his wife and Jonathan and he recognized Saul as the king anointed by God. But eventually he had to leave the land for his own survival and lived with his men by raiding villages. Yet when Saul and Jonathan died in battle with the Philistines, David lamented over both of them, honoring Saul as "mighty" and even "beloved and pleasant" (2 Samuel 1:17-27).

Multiple times David expressed his struggles in the psalms he wrote specifically in the context of being attacked by Saul (Psalms 18, 52, 54, 57, 59), but still returned to a place of glorifying God. Numerous other psalms expressed fear and anger toward his enemies and likely included Saul. Some were mostly crying out for help, pleading for justice, and calling for punishment. Yet, many included gratefulness for still being alive, praising God for deliverance, and in faith glorifying His name.

Discuss:

- How did Saul's actions and threats affect David?
  _____
  _____
  _____

- Why do you think David returned to Saul so many times and refused to hurt him? What role did the complexity of their relationship play?
  _____
  _____
  _____
  _____

- What sustained David during the years of running, hiding, and fighting? Consider his roots and relationships.
  _____
  _____
  _____

The Disease: Complex Trauma

Some trees collapse after their trunks become increasingly hollowed out by a resident disease or fungus, likely aided by

insects. Despite a tree's natural self-protective walls that usually form around a damaged area of the trunk, this disease had infiltrated it to the core and had eaten it from the inside.
Such a penetrating disease is far more dangerous than individual knots, with damage extending into the roots. It can represent compounded or "complex trauma" experienced in abusive relationships and long-term exposure to violence, which is particularly damaging for children.

Abuse

These ongoing patterns are much more common than we are aware of, or perhaps more than we would like to admit. There are many examples of a spiritual leader, such as a pastor, who looks pious on the outside. This causes people to trust him and feel valued when getting personal attention. Then he manipulates those who admire him into sexual relationships. Other times abuse within the home is downplayed or said to be biblical, a way of teaching the wife or child "submission" to the husband or parent.

There are five types of abuse:
- **Sexual:** This includes inappropriate touching, intercourse, and exposure to sexual actions or images. It compromises a beautiful form of intimacy, and survivors often struggle with shame, acceptance of their own body, and mistrust.
- **Physical:** This is injury that was not accidental, as well as threats and other forms of destruction. It leads to patterns of fear and feeling helpless.
- **Neglect:** This occurs when a child is not cared for, including practical needs (food, clothing, protection, etc.) and emotional needs. Children depend on their parents and can be deeply hurt when feeling no love from them.
- **Verbal/Emotional:** Words are very powerful and can be used to make someone feel worthless, helpless, and hopeless, especially when said by a parent or someone a child views as being in authority. Although not as visible

on the outside, the long-term effects can be just as damaging (sometime more) than physical hurt.
- **Spiritual:** When those in leadership or authority misuse Bible verses to manipulate others, contributing to unhealthy power over them and causing distorted views of God and the Bible. It usually employs verbal abuse.

Ongoing abuse is inflicted the majority of the time by someone close to the child, causing not only fear of the abuse itself, but confusion regarding the role of the individual that is supposed to be a source of care and security. Many times, children are too afraid to speak up, and if they do tell of what happened, other adults won't believe them. They may be disregarded or even threatened to avoid bringing shame to a family or a community. This is especially true when a leader or someone well-respected is involved. At other times, the blame is placed on the one being abused, who begins to believe that they are indeed in the wrong, bringing more unhealthy guilt and shame.

Because the effects go all the way to the roots, unhealthy patterns of attachment are created, which create poor templates for future relationships. The child does not learn how to set healthy boundaries or have a model for genuine love. Indeed, if not addressed similar patterns of abuse may occur in the next generation, when the victim becomes the perpetrator, just as a disease or fungus tends to spread if not halted.

Violence and Persecution

Numerous regions of today's world have been inundated by war after war, to the point where explosions, guns, and fleeing for safety become almost part of the "norm." In other places, people of different religions and ethnicities are being constantly estranged, harassed, captured, even tortured and killed. Like David, there is no end to the threat and no place to feel safe. Many of today's refugees come from such contexts, whether living in overcrowded camps or trying to adjust to a completely new setting: foreign in language, culture, and lifestyle. Too often the desperate need for care on emotional, spiritual, and relational levels is overlooked or ignored.

Discuss:

- What forms of abuse are you aware of in your community? Is there any unspoken acceptance or hiding of abusive patterns?

    _____
    _____
    _____

- How does your community respond to abuse? Do they take accusations against leaders seriously? Do they work to prevent the perpetrator from being back in a position of authority?

    _____
    _____
    _____
    _____

- What role should the church play in advocating for those constantly surrounded by oppression or violence? What about for those who have escaped and now need care and healing?

    _____
    _____
    _____

There are some situations toxic enough that a tree needs to be transplanted in order to survive. The destructive pattern of abuse is an example of a situation where intervention from the community is needed to stop the ugly "fungus," to reach out and stand up for the powerless. Some survivors are able to get out, but there needs to be a safe place for them to go, a place with healthy soil. At the same time, we cannot expect those caught in the trap of abuse, whether domestic or commercial, to free themselves. The manipulation used, whether through creating a financially/emotionally/physically dependent relationship or using fear, is truly tragic. To help someone break free, we must reach out to them in a loving, non-judgmental way.

As the Body of Christ, we have no excuse for failing to show love to those in deepest need. Jesus told his disciples that what they did for those hungry, thirsty, sick, needing shelter, or in prison was done for him. Likewise, failing to look after such people was the same as neglecting Him (Matthew 25:31-46). He also spoke specifically about caring for children, stating that, "Whoever receives one such child in My name receives Me; but whoever causes one of these little ones who believe in Me to stumble, it would be better for him to have a heavy millstone hung around his neck, and to be drown in the depth of the sea" (Matthew 18:5-6, NASB). If we are to love Christ, we need to be ready to help those most desperately in need of care, including the victims and survivors of abuse and persecution.

Take Home

Read: Isaiah 61:1-3

Reflect:

- Consider the list of people described: the afflicted, the brokenhearted, the captives, the prisoners, the grieving. What is the good news for these people? How do we deliver that good news?

  _____
  _____
  _____

- Imagine being in a place where persecution is a real life or death issue. Put yourself in the shoes of someone who faces abuse, but is too afraid to tell anyone.

- As you think of these individuals, do you find yourself experiencing any emotional reactions? Such emotions reflect compassion. Do you feel lacking in that or does it motivate you to take action?

  _____
  _____
  _____

Respond:

Look at the four means of showing love to the hurting and vulnerable and identify ways you could take action[5].
1. **Awareness:** Identify a specific group and do research to find out more about their needs.
2. **Prayer:** Set aside time to regularly intercede for this group based on the specific issues identified.
3. **Advocacy:** Speak up for the vulnerable who have no voice. Share what you've learned with your church, your community, and your leaders.

4. **Give:** Choose resources that you have, such as time, skills, and funds, to meet the needs of these individuals, whether in your own vicinity or through organizations that work across the globe.

- Make a decision now. What will you do?

    _____
    _____
    _____
    _____
    _____
    _____

The Tree of Life

Lesson 12: True Healing

Opening Question: Where do we look for healing of our emotional, spiritual, and relational wounds?

Jesus brings healing not only out of power, but out of love. Suffering comes as the result of sin, and Jesus came to pay the price for our sin. This sacrifice was part of God's big plan, foretold by Isaiah hundreds of years before the birth of Christ.

Bible Passage: Isaiah 53:1-6, NASB

> Who has believed our message?
>   And to whom has the arm of the Lord been revealed?
> For He grew up before Him like a tender shoot,
>   And like a root out of parched ground;
>   He has no stately form or majesty
>   That we should look upon Him,
>   Nor appearance that we should be attracted to Him.
> He was despised and forsaken of men,
>   A man of sorrows and acquainted with grief;
>   And like one from whom men hide their face
>   He was despised, and we did not esteem Him.
> Surely our griefs He Himself bore,
>   And our sorrows He carried;
>   Yet we ourselves esteemed Him stricken,
>   Smitten of God, and afflicted.
> But He was pierced through for our transgressions,
>   He was crushed for our iniquities;
>   The chastening for our well-being fell upon Him,
>   And by His scourging we are healed.
> All of us like sheep have gone astray,
>   Each of us has turned to his own way;
>   But the Lord has caused the iniquity of us all
>   To fall on Him.

Discuss:

- As you consider the suffering endured by Christ, how does that make you feel about your own struggles?

- What does it mean that we are healed by His scourging?

- Does Jesus understand what we endure from afar or does He relate to us from personal experience? How is that relevant to seeking healing from Him?

The Man at the Pool: Finding Healing in Jesus

When Jesus was in Jerusalem, He went by a pool where people jump in for healing when it is stirred up. That was an opportunity that only happened to one person at a time and not on a regular basis. There was a man debilitated enough that he could never make it into the pool in time and had no one to help him. This was no recent problem; he had been struggling for 38 years and Jesus knew it. How discouraging it must have been to be in that position day after day, year after year! Then, this man he didn't know asked him, "Do you wish to get well?" (John 5:6). What an absurd question, considering where he was! Or perhaps it felt judgmental, as if he hadn't put in enough effort or had enough faith to find healing. *I can't do it by myself; I've tried!*

Jesus didn't touch him, or even declare he was healed. He simply gave him instructions: "Get up, pick up your pallet and walk" (vs. 8). He was suddenly well, and immediately did what he was told, even though it went against the Sabbath day rules. His encounter with Jesus led to his healing and all other "laws" must have seemed insignificant next the life-changing miracle that occurred. He didn't know who Jesus was until later, when Jesus found him in the temple. Rather than tell him to offer sacrifices, Jesus invited him to leave the sin and brokenness in his life. Indeed, that was the deepest form of healing, possible only through Christ Himself. Lack of spiritual well-being was much more significant than his physical health.

Discuss:

- How would you feel if someone questioned your desire for healing from something you'd been struggling with for decades?

- Would you be ready to go against all societal norms to follow Jesus' instructions?

Capacity: How Deep Can You Dig?

After thinking through some possible problems that often start in our roots and may be related to loss and trauma, we may wonder if these are issues we can solve by ourselves, or perhaps with the help of a family member, church leader, or counselor. Indeed, some things can be improved as we learn ways to communicate better, become more aware of negative thought patterns, or study the Bible to learn more about accurate ways to perceive God. At the same time, it's very difficult to go into painful memories that need healing—in fact it's our natural defense to run away from them! Sometime progress can be made through working with a counselor or psychologist. Yet even there, we have a certain level of "capacity" to deal with the intensity of pain (including our physical reactions, our emotional reactions, and our spiritual reactions).[6]

Memories are created within our brains, influenced not just by what occurred, but also by the emotional and physical responses triggered in our bodies. In traumatic situations, our defense mechanisms are triggered by fear and the brain can't always process those memories in way that allows them to be accessed without feeling like it is happening all over again, including all the emotions. To find healing for those memories, we have to connect with that pain again while our brain processes the memory. The problem is, it can't be resolved if it is past a person's *capacity* to stay connected.[7]

The good news is that JESUS HAS INFINITE CAPACITY! By staying in His presence, we can press through painful memories we couldn't handle alone. The key is to remain connected with Him throughout the process. When using the Immanuel Intervention, the original positive memory and connection is a place we can always return to when feeling overwhelmed or losing that connection with Him.

Jesus also knows when our hearts and minds are *not* ready to address certain memories. Sometimes it's important to get more experience connecting with Him, learning to trust in and depend on Him, and see Him start to work in our lives. While we (whether the facilitator or the recipient) might feel the desire to get issues "solved," we must remember that God is the Gardener: we have to let Him be in charge and follow His guidance.

Discuss:

- If you've already experienced the Immanuel Intervention, were you able to connect with Jesus? If so, what was that like?

  _____
  _____
  _____

- Is there anything in your life that might be keeping you from connecting with Jesus or addressing particular memories? Consider issues like bitterness, sin, fear of facing hurt, traditional practices, or other hurdles. If so, ask Jesus to show you how to get past those blockages.

  _____
  _____
  _____
  _____

If you haven't yet had an Immanuel session, make sure to seek an opportunity to do so, and to become a facilitator yourself. But you don't need a formal session to seek Jesus and draw near to Him. That is something to do daily, taking time to be in His Presence and listen to Him.

Take Home

Read: John 5:1-15

Reflect:

- Picture yourself in the place of the man by the pool. You've been "stuck" in that place for a long time, but now this man comes to you, asking if you want healing.

- What issues have you dealt with for a long time that you would like to bring to Jesus? Consider relationships, habits, sins, worries, hurts, destructive patterns, doubts, and any other problems that came up over the course of this Bible Study.
  _____
  _____
  _____

- Listen to what Jesus says to you. He told the man to pick up his pallet and walk. What is He asking you to do?
  _____
  _____
  _____

Respond:

- Take what you felt Jesus wants you to do and choose concrete steps to take.
  1. _____
  2. _____
  3. _____

Conclusion

Hopefully this study has been an opportunity to see places for healing in your own life and ways to help others find healing in their lives. Take time to review your discussions and reflections, and to write down what you want to take with you.

I learned…

_____
_____
_____
_____
_____
_____
_____
_____

I want to respond by…

_____
_____
_____
_____
_____
_____
_____
_____

The Tree of Life

Appendix A: The Immanuel Approach

The "Immanuel Approach" was developed by Dr. Karl Lehman. It is founded on biblical principles, while integrating what we know about our brains and our response to trauma.

Jesus arrived in human form, introduced as Immanuel, "God with us," a bridge between a holy God and sinful humanity. As the name implies, and we can learn to be more aware of **His presence** and in tune with Him. The more we are in a deeper relationship with Christ, the more we can see His hand at work. The more we come into His presence, the more we can see His face. It is centered on our relationship with Him. There we find healing and wholeness.

Dr. Lehman writes: *"Our ultimate goal with the Immanuel approach for life is getting to the place where we perceive the Lord's presence, and abide in an interactive connection with Jesus, as our usual, normal, baseline condition as we walk through life each day."* [8]

It is called an "approach" because, as Lehman describes, it is not just for traumatic situations, it is for a way of life. Just as a tree absorbs water and light for life, being in the Presence of the Lord with His living water flowing through us brings growth and restoration. ***The overall goal is drawing nearer to Jesus.***

Immanuel Intervention: Seeing Jesus in the Trauma

This Bible Study has suggested practicing "Immanuel Interventions," which are *"specific, focused, systematic interventions with the goal of helping the perceiving ministry to perceive the Lord's living presence, and to establish an adequate interactive connection with Him."* [9] It is for addressing painful memories, encountering Jesus in those memories, and receiving His healing. The basic outline is provided here for reference. Hopefully it is being incorporated by a facilitator who has completed the full training.

Steps to Facilitate Connecting with Jesus

If this is the first time you have met the recipient, take time to introduce yourself and the Immanuel Approach, including the significance of "God with us" and the value of being able experience His Presence. Ask if they would be interested in trying it, and describe the basic idea of being a conversation with Jesus, not with you; you are just present to facilitate the process.

(The bold text can provide specific words to say, but variations are fine as you become more comfortable.)

1. Remembering a positive event

Think of a specific positive memory when you felt joy and perceived the Lord's presence.

If they are struggling to remember a time, ask if there was a time they remember feeling happy or joyful.

If they only tell of a general memory of being aware God is always around us: ***Choose one time when you remember encountering God.***

Spend a few minutes reentering that event (remembering where you were, who was there, what you were doing), while I open this time in prayer.

After dedicating time to the Lord, encourage them to stay in that memory, keeping their eyes closed.

As you are in that place, ask Jesus to show you where He is at that time. Share with me whatever comes to mind, whether pictures, words, or feelings.

(Developed by Karl Lehman. Adapted by Emily Hervey.)

2. Appreciating God's presence

(After they have shared): **Take a minute to express your appreciation to God for His Presence and the way He showed Himself in that memory.**

(After they have prayed): **What emotions are you feeling?**

If they describe only positive emotions move on to the next step.

3. Connecting with Jesus in the present

Where is Jesus right now? Encourage them to look for His physical presence.

Ask Him to show you whatever He wants you to know.

If they stay silent for some time, ask what is going through their mind, whether pictures, words, or feelings. If there are any areas of confusion, when they don't understand what something means, say, *"Ask Jesus what it means."*

Make sure they are in a place of feeling peace and joy before closing the time.

4. Response to Jesus and closing.

Open your heart to Him, responding to whatever He showed you.

When they are done, either close in prayer, thanking God for the specific ways He showed Himself, or ask if they are ready to proceed to a painful memory (step 5).

(Developed by Karl Lehman. Adapted by Emily Hervey.)

Steps to Facilitate Encountering Jesus in the Trauma

5. *Think back to the painful memory.*

   Remember the painful event, allowing yourself to be there again. You don't have to tell me all the details, but let me know what is going on at this time.

6. *Invite Jesus into that memory.*

   Ask Jesus where He was in that memory.

(When connecting with Him and describing what He was doing:) **Interact with Him, asking what He wants you to know, responding to what you see/hear/feel, asking for help as you need it.**

You may need to give prompts along the way when they are "stuck" or are not sure of what something means. Always point them back to Jesus: e.g. *"Ask Jesus what's getting in the way"* or

"Tell Jesus what you're struggling with right now."

*If they cannot connect with Jesus in that memory, if they lose that connection, or if it's close to time to end, always go back to the safety net, connecting with Jesus as done at the beginning. Never stop the session when the recipient is feeling overwhelmed by negative emotions.

7. *Check emotions. When all positive, end by expressing appreciation to Jesus and responding to whatever He did.*

   Tell Jesus anything else you want to, and take time for appreciation. Then I will close in prayer.

When praying to end the session, give thanks for the specific ways that the recipient connected with Jesus and found healing, declare His victory, ask for continued blessing, and anything the Holy Spirit prompts you to say

(Developed by Karl Lehman. Adapted by Emily Hervey.)

Notes

[1] Adapted from Helpguide.org: Trusted guide to mental & emotional health, *"Helping Someone Who's Grieving."*
https://www.helpguide.org/articles/grief/helping-someone-who-is-grieving.htm

[2] American Psychiatric Association. (2013) Diagnostic and Statistical Manual of Mental Disorders, (5th edition).

[3] Psychological First Aid Field Operations Guide, 2nd Edition

[4] American Psychiatric Association. (2013) Diagnostic and Statistical Manual of Mental Disorders, (5th edition).

[5] Based on "Heirloom Love: Authentic Christianity in This Age of Persecution," by Dominic Sputo.

[6] The concept of capacity has been developed and discussed by James Wilder and Karl Lehman.

[7] See Wilder, E. J. (1999). *The Red Dragon Cast Down* and http://www.lifemodel.org/

[8] Karl Lehman, http://www.immanuelapproach.com/pdf/ImmAppRevisitPOSTShrt.pdf

[9] Taken from "Brain Science, Psychological Trauma, & the God Who Is with Us," K.D. Lehman, 2007.

Made in the USA
Middletown, DE
26 September 2023

39472371R00057